PRIMARY CLASSIC

Goldilocks
and the
Three Bears

Adapted for ELT by Joanne Swan

NEW EDITIONS
English Language Teaching

English Language Teaching edition first published by New Editions 2004

New Editions
37 Bagley Wood Road
Kennington
Oxford OX1 5LY
England

New Editions
PO Box 76101
17110 Nea Smyrni
Athens
Greece

Tel: (+30) 210 9883156
Fax: (+30) 210 9880223
E-mail: enquiries@new-editions.com
Website: www.new-editions.com

For this English Language Teaching edition © New Editions 2004

Original Spanish title: Ricitos de Oro y los Tres Osos
Original Edition © Parramon Ediciones SA, Barcelona, España
World rights reserved

ISBN 960-403-200-3

Recording and production at GFS-PRO Studio by George Flamouridis

Contents

This is the story of a little girl. Her name is Goldilocks. She's got golden hair. Everyone loves her. Every day she goes to the village.

'Hello, Goldilocks! How are you?' everyone asks.

Goldilocks smiles and says, 'I'm fine. How are you?'

Goldilocks is eating her dinner with her mother. She asks, 'Why is the forest bad, Mother?'

'There are dangerous animals in the forest, Goldilocks. Don't go there!' says her mother.

But Goldilocks wants to go there. She wants to see the animals. She wants to see the trees and flowers in the forest. She thinks about the forest every day.

The next day, Goldilocks talks to her mother.

'Mother, I'm going to Alice's house,' she says.

But Goldilocks isn't going to Alice's house.
She is going to the forest!

The blacksmith sees her and he says,
'Hello, Goldilocks. Where are you going?'

But Goldilocks doesn't say anything.
She walks quickly out of the village.

She goes into the forest. She sees green
trees, beautiful birds and butterflies.
She sees a squirrel and a rabbit.

'It's a beautiful forest!' she says.
'It isn't dangerous!'

Goldilocks plays with the animals. She looks at the beautiful trees and flowers.

After an hour, Goldilocks is hungry and thirsty. She sees a house in the forest.

'I can get water there,' she thinks.

She walks to the house and knocks on the door.

She listens for a minute and she opens the door. The house is nice and tidy. She looks in the kitchen. There is a table. There are three bowls of soup on the table. Goldilocks is hungry. She wants to eat the soup.

Goldilocks eats some soup from the first bowl. It's very hot! She eats some soup from the second bowl. It's very cold! She eats some soup from the third bowl. It's very good. She eats all the soup.

Now Goldilocks is tired. She wants to sleep.

She goes to the bedroom. There are three beds. The first bed is very big. The second bed is very old. The third bed is very nice. Goldilocks sleeps in the third bed.

Later, three brown bears come into the house. They live there. Every day before lunch, they walk in the forest.

'My spoon is dirty!' says Father Bear.

'My spoon is dirty!' says Mother Bear.

'My spoon is dirty, and where's my soup?' asks Baby Bear.

'Who is in our house?' asks Father Bear.

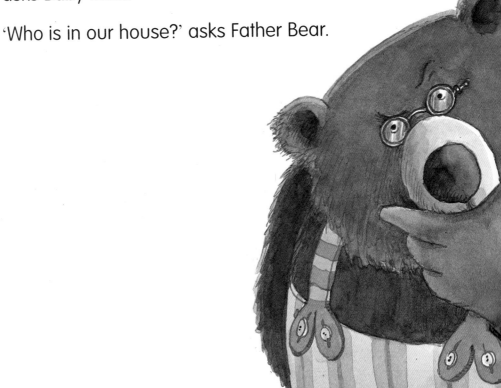

The bears go into the bedroom.

'My bed isn't tidy!' says Father Bear.

'My bed isn't tidy!' says Mother Bear.

'My bed isn't tidy and there's a girl in it!' says Baby Bear.

'Who are you?' asks Father Bear.

Goldilocks hears the bears. She wakes up. She sees the three brown bears next to her. 'Help!' she shouts.

'What are you doing here?' asks
Father Bear.

'Are ... are you dangerous animals?'
asks Goldilocks.

'Dangerous? Oh no, we aren't dangerous,'
says Mother Bear.

'We're good bears,' says Baby bear.

Goldilocks is crying. She wants to go home.

'I want to go home,' she says. 'I want
my mother!'

Mother Bear is very nice.

She says, 'Don't cry, little girl. Baby Bear can take you to the village.'

Goldilocks and Baby Bear leave.
They walk quickly in the forest. They see the village.

'Please come into the forest again,' says Baby Bear. 'We can play.'

Goldilocks's mother is looking for her.

'Oh, there you are, Goldilocks!' she says.

She smiles and kisses Goldilocks. She is
very happy to see her.

Goldilocks tells her mother about the bears.

'They aren't dangerous, Mother. I want to go and play with them again,' she says.

Every day, Goldilocks says to her mother, 'I'm going into the forest. I want to play with Baby Bear.'

Her mother doesn't believe her but she smiles and says, 'Yes, OK.'

Now Goldilocks and Baby Bear are very good friends. They play every day.

Activities

Activities

 **Match.**

a

b

c

1 squirrel
2 rabbit
3 bowl
4 flowers
5 bed
6 spoon

d

e

f

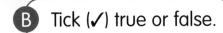 **Tick (✓) true or false.**

	T	F
1 Goldilocks has got brown hair.		
2 The forest is beautiful.		
3 There are five bowls of soup on the table.		
4 Goldilocks sleeps in the third bed.		
5 Goldilocks's mother kisses her.		
6 Goldilocks doesn't play with Baby Bear.		

C Write.

> big   forest   golden   happy
> house   lunch   plays   nice

1 Goldilocks has got .... hair.
2 Goldilocks goes into the ....
3 Goldilocks sees a .... in the forest.
4 The first bed is very ....
5 Every day before ...., the bears walk
   in the forest.
6 Mother Bear is very ....
7 Goldilocks's mother is .... to see her.
8 Goldilocks .... with Baby Bear
   every day.

```
1 [ ][ ][ ][ ] S
      2 [ ] L [ ][ ][ ]
  3 [ ][ ][ ][ ] E [ ]
    4 [ ][ ][ ] E [ ][ ][ ]
        5 P [ ][ ]
        6 S [ ][ ]
```

1 The three ..... live in the forest.
2 Baby Bear takes Goldilocks to the ..... .
3 Goldilocks looks in the ..... .
4 The bears aren't ..... .
5 Baby Bear wants to ..... with Goldilocks.
6 Goldilocks eats Baby Bear's ..... .

E Find.

animals   beautiful   bedroom   bowl
dangerous   forest   kitchen
soup   squirrel   village

```
B  E  A  U  T  I  F  U  L
V  F  O  R  E  S  T  K  D
I  C  N  E  N  Q  A  I  A
L  E  A  L  Q  U  N  T  N
L  S  O  V  T  I  I  C  G
A  O  L  A  K  R  M  H  E
G  U  T  N  R  R  A  E  R
E  P  N  T  L  E  L  N  O
T  H  B  O  W  L  S  R  U
H  B  E  D  R  O  O  M  S
```

F Colour.

Picture Glossary

bear

blacksmith

bowl

butterfly

cry

forest

hair

smile

spoon

squirrel

village

walk